BOSTON COMMON PRESS
Brookline, Massachusetts

1998

Boston Common Press
17 Station Street
Brookline, Massachusetts 02146

ISBN 0-936184-24-8
Library of Congress Cataloging-in-Publication Data
The Editors of *Cook's Illustrated*
    How to make salad: An illustrated step-by-step guide to perfect salads and dressings/The Editors of *Cook's Illustrated*
1st ed.

    Includes 56 recipes and 39 illustrations
    ISBN 0-936184-24-8 (hardback): $14.95
    I. Cooking. I. Title
1998

Manufactured in the United States of America

Distributed by Boston Common Press, 17 Station Street, Brookline, MA 02146.

Cover and text design by Amy Klee
Recipe development by Melissa Hamilton
Series Editor: Jack Bishop

HOW
TO MAKE
SALAD

An illustrated step-by-step guide to
perfect salads and dressings.

THE COOK'S ILLUSTRATED LIBRARY

Illustrations by John Burgoyne

CONTENTS

introduction

O

NE MIGHT ASK, "WHY WRITE A BOOK
about making salads?" It would appear a
rather straightforward task; nothing more
than a few greens and a simple dressing.
Yet, as is often true in cooking, the simplest recipes are in
fact the hardest. Making a proper vinaigrette is not as simple as three parts oil to one part vinegar. It turns out that a
higher ratio of oil to vinegar is best for most of the high-acid
vinegars on the market today and the notion of adding oil in
a thin stream, almost drop by drop, is simply unnecessary.

There is also plenty of science to creating the perfect
mayonnaise. Unlike a vinaigrette, in which the vinegar is
dispersed into the oil, a mayonnaise is formed by breaking
down the oil into tiny droplets that are bound together by
the lemon juice and egg yolks. What makes a mayonnaise
so interesting is that three-quarters of a cup of oil is con-
tained by a mere two tablespoons of yolk and lemon juice.
Unlike a vinaigrette, the whisking must be done thoroughly and the oil added slowly to achieve the proper result.

For the salads themselves, we have tested different methods and potatoes for making the perfect potato salad, investigated the secrets of a creamy Caesar salad (the egg must be coddled), and found that salting cabbage before making coleslaw solves the problem of a watery dressing. We also have provided plenty of carefully tested recipes for main course, vegetable, grain, and bean salads.

We have also published *How to Make Pasta Sauces*, *How to Make Holiday Desserts*, *How to Make a Pie*, *How to Make an American Layer Cake*, *How to Stir-Fry*, *How to Make Ice Cream*, and *How to Make Pizza*, and many other titles in this series will soon be available. To order other books, call us at (800) 611-0759. We are also the editors and publishers of *Cook's Illustrated*, a bimonthly publication about American home cooking. For a free trial copy of *Cook's*, call (800) 526-8442.

Christopher P. Kimball
Publisher and Editor
Cook's Illustrated

chapter one

≋

SALAD BASICS

AKING SALAD IS ONE OF THE MOST CRE-
ative culinary pursuits. Baking requires
that the cook follow directions precisely.
Roasting a chicken or cooking pasta
also demands a high level of attention to detail. But salad
making allows for a fair amount of improvisation.
Watercress can be substituted for arugula, which in turn can
be substituted for dandelion greens or mizuna. If you like
bell peppers, cucumbers, or tomatoes, they can be added to
almost any salad.

Salad making is creative, but there are some broad
guidelines that must be followed to achieve optimal results.

▪▪ SHOP CAREFULLY. Most greens have a short shelf-life, so it's especially important to buy specimens that look healthy at the market. Greens with stems and roots will stay fresher longer and should be purchased when possible. Also, look for any rot among bunches as you shop. Decay can spread quickly and it's best to avoid greens on which this process has already begun. If you get greens home and notice a few slimy leaves, pick them out immediately rather than waiting until you make salad. If you wait, the rot may well have spread throughout the bunch.

▪▪ KEEP CRISP. Because they are mostly water, greens should be stored in the crisper drawer of the refrigerator, where the humidity is the highest. But while moist air will help prolong their freshness, excessive amounts of water won't. Therefore, don't wash lettuces until you are ready to use them and drain off any standing water in bags before refrigerating greens.

▪▪ WASH AND DRY THOROUGHLY. Because they grow in such close proximity to the ground, salad greens are often quite sandy. Thorough washing in a deep bowl or sink filled with cold water is a must. Swish the greens in the water to loosen any sand. Once the bottom of bowl is free of grit (you may need to drain the bowl and add clean water several times), dry greens in a salad spinner and then use paper or kitchen towels to blot off any remaining moisture. It's imperative to remove all visible moisture. Dressing will slide off damp greens and pool up at the bottom of the salad bowl. Washed and dried greens can be refrigerated in a dry zipper-lock bag for several hours.

▪▪ DON'T TEAR UNTIL READY TO EAT. While whole leaves can be washed and dried in advance, do not tear lettuces until ready to dress the salad. Tearing the leaves leads to oxidation and browning in delicate greens. Whatever you do, don't take a knife to salad greens. The more violently they are cut, the quicker they will brown. Gentle tearing of large leaves by hand is best.

▪▪ DRESS GREENS LIGHTLY. Nothing is worse than a limp, soggy salad with too much dressing. Dressed greens should glisten. We find that ¼ cup of vinaigrette is sufficient to dress 2 quarts of salad greens, enough for four servings. We lightly pack a 4-cup plastic measure to portion out greens.

▪▪ SERVE IMMEDIATELY. Once a salad is dressed, the clock is ticking. Waiting even 15 minutes to eat the salad may cause some loss in freshness and crispness. The longer salad greens sit under a coating of a dressing, the less appetizing they become as the salt in the dressing draws moisture out of the greens and causes them to become limp.

GLOSSARY OF SALAD GREENS

The following list starts with the four main varieties of lettuce and then covers the most commonly available specialty greens. When substituting one green for another, try to choose greens with a similar intensity. For example, peppery arugula could be used as a substitute for watercress or dandelion greens, but not for red leaf lettuce, at least not without significantly altering the flavor of the salad. Figures 1 through 4 on pages 16 and 17 offer some general guidelines on substitutions.

BUTTERHEAD LETTUCES: Boston and Bibb are the two most common varieties of these very mild-tasting lettuces. A head of butterhead lettuce has a nice round shape and loose outer leaves. The color of the leaves is light to medium green (except, of course, in red-tinged varieties) and the leaves are extremely tender.

LOOSELEAF LETTUCES: Red leaf, green leaf, red oak, and lolla rossa are the most common varieties. These lettuces grow in a loose rosette shape, not a tight head. The ruffled leaves are green at the base and magenta toward the top in red varieties. These lettuces are the perhaps most versatile because their texture is soft yet still a bit crunchy and their flavor is mild but not bland.

ROMAINE LETTUCE: The leaves on this lettuce are long and broad at the top. The color shades from dark green in outer leaves (which are often tough and should be discarded) to pale green in the thick, crisp heart. Also called Cos lettuce, this variety has more crunch than either butterhead or looseleaf lettuces and a more pronounced earthy flavor. Romaine lettuce is essential in Caesar salad, when the greens must stand up to a thick, creamy dressing.

ICEBERG LETTUCE: Iceberg is the best known variety of crisphead lettuce. Its shape is perfectly round and the leaves are tightly packed. A high water content makes iceberg especially crisp and crunchy, but also robs it of flavor.

ARUGULA: Also called rocket, this tender, dark green leaf can be faintly peppery or downright spicy. Larger, older leaves tend to be hotter than small, young leaves, but the flavor is variable, so taste arugula before adding it to a salad. Try to buy arugula in bunches with the stems and roots still attached—they help keep the leaves fresh. Arugula bruises and discolors quite easily. Try to keep stemmed leaves whole. Very large leaves can be torn just before they are needed.

WATERCRESS: With its small leaves and long, thick stalks, watercress is easy to spot. It requires some patience in the kitchen because the stalks are really quite tough and must be removed one at a time. The leaves are usually mildly spicy, like arugula.

DANDELION GREENS: Dandelion greens are tender and pleasantly bitter. The leaves are long and have ragged edges. The flavor is similar to that of arugula or watercress, both of which can be used interchangeably with dandelion. Note that tougher, older leaves that are more than several inches long should be cooked and not used raw in salads.

MIZUNA: This Japanese spider mustard has long, thin, dark green leaves with deeply cut jagged edges. Sturdier than arugula, watercress, or dandelion, it can nonetheless be used interchangeably with these slightly milder greens in salads when a strong peppery punch is desired. Note that larger, older leaves are better cooked, so choose small "baby" mizuna for salads.

TATSOI: This Asian green has thin white stalks and round, dark green leaves. A member of the crucifer family of vegetables that includes broccoli and cabbages, tatsoi tastes like a mild Chinese cabbage, especially bok choy. However, the texture of these miniature leaves is always delicate.

RADICCHIO: This most familiar chicory was almost unknown

in this country two decades ago. The tight heads of purple leaves streaked with prominent white ribs are now a supermarket staple. Radicchio has a decent punch but is not nearly as bitter as other chicories, especially Belgian endive.

BELGIAN ENDIVE: With its characteristic bitter chicory flavor, endive is generally used sparingly in salads. Unlike its cousin radicchio, endive is crisp and crunchy, not tender and leafy. The yellow leaf tips are usually mild-flavored, while the white, thick leaf bases are more bitter. Endive is the one salad green we routinely cut rather than tear. Remove whole leaves from the head and then slice crosswise into bite-sized pieces.

CHICORY: Chicory, or curly endive, has curly, cut leaves that form a loose head that resembles a sunburst. The leaves are bright green and their flavor is usually fairly bitter. The outer leaves can be somewhat tough, especially at the base. Inner leaves are generally more tender.

ESCAROLE: Escarole has smooth, broad leaves bunched together in a loose head. With its long ribs and softly ruffled leaves, it looks a bit like leaf lettuce. As a member of the chicory family, the flavor can be intense, although not nearly as strong as that of endive or chicory.

FRISÉE: This spiky, miniature green has a nutty, almost buttery flavor as well as the characteristic bitterness of all chicories. Although the leaves are quite thin, they are not as soft as they seem and provide a fairly good crunch.

SPINACH: Of all the cooking greens, this one is the most versatile in salads because it can be used in its miniature or full-grown form. Flat-leaf spinach is better than curly-leaf spinach in salads because the stems are usually less fibrous and the spade-shaped leaves are thinner, more tender, and sweeter. Curly spinach is often dry and chewy, while flat-leaf spinach, sold in bundles rather than in cellophane bags, is usually tender and moist, more like lettuce than a cooking green.

BABY COOKING GREENS: Miniature versions of chard, beet greens, turnip greens, and kale are often sold separately by the pound at supermarkets or used in salad mixes like mesclun. The white- or red-veined leaves are easy to spot. The flavor is much milder than that of full-sized cooking greens.

Figure 1.

Tender, mild leaf lettuces are the most commonly available salad greens. Although they can be used alone, they work well when mixed with stronger-tasting greens. Lettuces from left to right, red leaf, iceberg, Boston, and Romaine.

Figure 2.

Tender, peppery dark greens add punch to any salad. They are often mixed with milder greens, but can stand alone in refreshing palate-cleansing salads. From left to right, watercress, dandelion, arugula, tatsoi, and mizuna.

16

Figure 3.
The chicory family includes many different-looking salad greens.
Most are somewhat bitter and crunchy. From left to right,
radicchio, Belgian endive, chicory, escarole, and frisée.

Figure 4.
Sturdier "cooking" greens are often used in salads. Full-sized leaves
of spinach, the mildest and most tender of these greens, can be used
in salads, as well as baby spinach. Otherwise, only very young
leaves such as baby beet and chard greens are appropriate in salads.
From left to right, baby spinach, baby red Swiss chard, baby kale,
baby broccoli rabe, baby carrot tops, and baby beet greens.

17

chapter two

≩

DRESSINGS

THERE ARE TWO TYPES OF COLD SAUCES typically used to dress salads. Vinaigrette is a relatively thin emulsion made of oil, vinegar, and seasonings. Mayonnaise is a thick, creamy emulsion of egg yolk and oil with a little acid and some seasonings.

An emulsion is a mixture of two things that don't ordinarily mix, such as oil and water, or oil and vinegar. The only way to mix them is to stir or whisk so strenuously that the two ingredients break down into tiny droplets. Many of these droplets will continue to find each other and recoalesce into pure fluid. (This is what happens when the emulsion breaks.) Eventually one of the fluids (usually the less plentiful one) will break entirely into droplets so tiny that they remain separated by the opposite fluid, at least temporarily.

The liquid in the droplet form is called the dispersed phase because the droplets are dispersed throughout the emulsion. The liquid that surrounds the droplets is the continuous phase. Because the continuous phase forms the surface of the emulsion, that's what the mouth and tongue feel and taste first.

Vinaigrette is the most common dressing for salads, used with leafy greens as well as vegetables, grains, and beans. While it is possible to dress a salad with oil and then vinegar, the results are quite different when these ingredients are combined before being poured over greens.

To demonstrate this difference, try this test. Dress a simple green salad first with oil, then a mixture of vinegar, salt, and pepper. The result will be harsh, with an extremely prominent vinegar bite. Next, take another batch of greens and the same dressing ingredients. Mix the salt and pepper into the vinegar and then whisk in the oil until the dressing is translucent. When this emulsified dressing is poured over greens, the flavor will be smoother with a greater emphasis on the oil.

The science of emulsions explains why the same ingredients can taste so different. In the first oil-then-vinegar salad, the oil and vinegar don't mix, so both race up the tongue. The less viscous vinegar wins, hence this salad tastes more acidic. In the emulsion, the oil is whipped into tiny molecules that surround dispersed droplets of vinegar. The oil is the continuous phase and is tasted first. Your tongue is coated with fat droplets that cushion the impact of the acid.

The correct ratio of oil to vinegar is open to much discussion and can depend on the acidity of the vinegar as well as the flavor of the oil. In general, we prefer a ratio of four parts oil to one part acid, but this can vary, especially when using citrus juices and rice wine vinegar, which are much less acidic than common vinegars.

In terms of forming a vinaigrette, either a fork or small whisk will generate the whipping action necessary to break up the oil into small droplets. With either tool, the emulsion will break rather quickly so rewhisk the dressing just before pouring it over salad greens. We found that adding the salt and pepper to the vinegar is best because the vinegar mutes these flavors a bit and prevents them from becoming too overpowering. On the other hand, we prefer to add herbs and some other seasonings to the finished dressing to maximize their impact.

Mayonnaise is used to dress vegetable salads—especially potato salad and coleslaw. It acts as a creamy binder and adds richness to any salad. The science of mayonnaise is fairly complex and unusual. Whisking transforms three thin liquids—vegetable oil, lemon juice, and egg yolk—into a thick, creamy sauce. In this sauce, the egg yolk and lemon juice are the continuous phase (that's why something that is 95 percent oil doesn't taste greasy) and the oil is the dispersed phase that must be broken into tiny droplets.

Mayonnaise works because an egg yolk is such a good emulsifier and stabilizer. But sometimes mayonnaise can "break," as the ingredients revert back to their original liquid form. To keep mayonnaise from breaking, it is first necessary to whisk the egg yolk and lemon juice thoroughly (the egg yolk itself contains liquid and fat materials that must be emulsified). It is equally important to add the oil slowly to the egg yolk. Remember, two tablespoons of yolk and lemon juice must be "stretched" around ¾ cup of oil.

In terms of oil, we like the flavor of corn oil in our basic mayonnaise. It produces a dressing that is rich and eggy with good body. Canola oil makes a slightly lighter, more lemony mayo. We find that extra-virgin olive oil can be harsh and bitter, especially if used alone in mayonnaise. Pure olive oil produces a mellower mayonnaise but is more costly than corn or canola oil and does not deliver better results.

While homemade mayonnaise is a delicious addition to salads, many cooks prefer the convenience and safety of commercial brands made without raw eggs. In our tasting of major brands, Hellmann's came out on top. Among light or reduced-calorie brands, Hellmann's again beat out Kraft, which is its main competition in the marketplace.

GLOSSARY OF OILS AND VINEGARS

The following oils and vinegars are used in recipes throughout this book. To keep oils from becoming rancid, store bottles in a cool, dark pantry and buy small quantities that will be used up within a few months. Storing oils in the refrigerator will prolong their freshness.

EXTRA-VIRGIN OLIVE OIL: This is our standard choice for most salads. In blind tastings, we could not tell the difference between extra-virgin oil that cost $10 per liter and $80 per liter. However, cheaper pure and "light" oils are characterless and decidedly inferior in salads, although they may be fine for some cooking. An inexpensive supermarket extra-virgin oil, such as Berio or Colavita, is our recommendation for salads.

WALNUT OIL: This oil has a warm, nutty flavor that works well in salads with fruits and/or toasted nuts. Like other nut oils, walnut oil tends to go rancid quickly and is best stored in the refrigerator.

ASIAN SESAME OIL: With its dark brown color and rich aroma, toasted sesame oil adds a distinctive Asian flavor to salad dressings. Use it in moderation. More than a tablespoon or so will overwhelm other ingredients.

CANOLA OIL: This bland oil is best used to soften a particularly strong oil, especially sesame or walnut. Alone, its flavor is unremarkable. But in combination with a potent nut or seed oil, canola can be part of a good dressing.

RED WINE VINEGAR: Red wine vinegar is the most versatile choice in salads. Its flavor is sharp but clean. Domestic brands tend to have an acidity around 5 percent, while imported red brands often contain as much as 7 percent. In our tasting of red wine vinegars, Heinz beat other domestic brands as well as imports, some of which cost ten times as much.

WHITE WINE VINEGAR: Similar to red wine vinegar but often not quite as complex. Our choice when a pink vinaigrette made with red wine vinegar might seem odd.

BALSAMIC VINEGAR: A rich, sweet, oaky vinegar that is best used in combination with red wine vinegar in salads. Real balsamic vinegar is aged many years and costs at least $10 per bottle. Cheap supermarket versions are nothing more than caramel-colored red wine vinegar. They are usually harsh and unpleasant tasting. Given the small quantities of balsamic vinegar needed to transform a salad, it's worth investing in the real thing. In our tasting, we liked vinegars from Cavalli, Fiorucci, Fini, and Masserie di Sant'Eramo.

SHERRY VINEGAR: This Spanish vinegar is usually quite strong (often with 7 percent acidity) but has a rich, oaky, nutty flavor.

CITRUS JUICES: Orange, lime, and lemon juices can all be used in salad dressing. They add acidity as well as flavor. Lemon and lime juices are more acidic and can stand on their own. Orange juice is usually combined with vinegar. To add more citrus flavor without disturbing the ratio of acid to oil, stir in some grated zest.

RICE WINE VINEGAR: A natural choice in Asian dressings, this low-acidity (about 4.5 percent), clear vinegar is quite mild. Use it when you want to keep acidity in check but want to avoid the distinctive flavor of citrus juices.

♛

Master Recipe

Classic Vinaigrette

➤ **NOTE:** *Salt and pepper are mixed first with the vinegar for subtlety. If you like, you can adjust the seasonings after the salad has been dressed by sprinkling additional salt and/or pepper directly onto the greens. The Master Recipe makes about ½ cup, enough to dress 4 quarts (or eight servings) of leafy salad. Extra dressing can be refrigerated for up to a week. Variations that contain fresh herbs should be used within several hours for maximum freshness.*

1½	tablespoons red wine vinegar
¼	teaspoon salt
⅛	teaspoon ground black pepper
6	tablespoons extra-virgin olive oil

⠿ INSTRUCTIONS:

Combine vinegar, salt, and pepper in bowl with fork. Add oil, then whisk or mix with fork until smooth, about 30 seconds. The dressing will separate after 5 or 10 minutes, so use immediately or cover and refrigerate for several days and mix again before tossing with greens.

Mediterranean Vinaigrette

Replace vinegar with 2¼ teaspoons lemon juice, increase pepper to ¼ teaspoon, and decrease oil to 4 tablespoons. Whisk 1 tablespoon drained and minced capers, 1 tablespoon minced fresh parsley leaves, 1 teaspoon minced fresh thyme leaves, and 1 medium garlic clove, minced fine, into finished dressing.

Balsamic Vinaigrette

Reduce red wine vinegar to 1½ teaspoons and combine with 1½ tablespoons balsamic vinegar.

Walnut Vinaigrette

Replace vinegar with 2 tablespoons lemon juice and replace olive oil with 4 tablespoons canola oil mixed with 2 tablespoons walnut oil.

Mixed Herb Vinaigrette

Add 1 tablespoon minced fresh basil leaves, 1½ teaspoons minced fresh parsley leaves, and 1 teaspoon minced fresh oregano leaves to finished dressing. Use dressing within several hours for optimum freshness.

Shallot Vinaigrette

Add 1 tablespoon minced shallot to vinegar, salt, and pepper. Let stand 10 minutes. Whisk in oil and use dressing within several hours for optimum freshness.

Basil-Curry Vinaigrette

Replace red wine vinegar with 1½ tablespoons each lemon juice and white wine vinegar. Combine lemon juice, vinegar, salt, and pepper with ½ teaspoon curry powder and 1½ teaspoons honey. Reduce oil to 4 tablespoons. Whisk 3 tablespoons minced fresh basil leaves into finished dressing. Use dressing within several hours for optimum freshness.

Creamy Vinaigrette

Replace red wine vinegar with 1 tablespoon white wine vinegar. Combine vinegar, salt, and pepper with 1 tablespoon lemon juice and 2 teaspoons Dijon-style mustard. Reduce oil to 4 tablespoons. Whisk 2 tablespoons sour cream or plain yogurt into finished dressing. This recipe yields ⅔ cup dressing.

Orange-Sesame Vinaigrette

Replace red wine vinegar with 1 tablespoon rice wine vinegar. Combine vinegar, salt, and pepper with 1 teaspoon grated orange zest, 2 tablespoons orange juice, and 1 tablespoon minced fresh gingerroot. Replace olive oil with 4 tablespoons canola oil mixed with 1 tablespoon Asian sesame oil. This recipe yields ⅔ cup dressing.

Tarragon-Mustard Vinaigrette

Replace red wine vinegar with 2 tablespoons white wine

vinegar. Increase salt to ½ teaspoon and pepper to ¼ teaspoon. Combine vinegar, salt, and pepper with 1 tablespoon Dijon-style mustard and 1 tablespoon minced fresh tarragon leaves. Whisk in oil and use dressing within several hours for optimum freshness. This recipe yields ⅔ cup dressing.

Orange Vinaigrette

Decrease red wine vinegar to 2 teaspoons. Combine vinegar, salt, and pepper with 1 teaspoon minced orange zest and 4 tablespoons orange juice. Increase olive oil to ½ cup. This recipe yields ¾ cup dressing.

Hoisin Vinaigrette

Replace red wine vinegar with ⅓ cup rice wine vinegar and omit salt and pepper. Combine vinegar with 1½ tablespoons soy sauce, 3 tablespoons hoisin sauce, and 1 tablespoon minced fresh gingerroot. Replace olive oil with 3 tablespoons canola oil mixed with 1 tablespoon Asian sesame oil. This recipe yields ¾ cup dressing.

Figure 5.
Shallots add spark to many dressings. To keep them from over-powering other ingredients, they must be minced quite fine. Start by placing the peeled bulb flat side down on a work surface and slicing crosswise almost to (but not through) the root end.

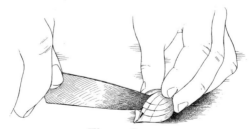

Figure 6.
Make a number of parallel cuts through the top of the shallot down to the work surface.

Figure 7.
Finally, make very thin slices perpendicular to the lengthwise
cuts made in figure 6.

Figure 8.
We have tested numerous methods for extracting as much juice as
possible from lemons (and limes) and have devised the following
method. Start by rolling the lemon on a hard surface, pressing
down firmly with the palm of your hand.

Figure 9.
Cut the fruit in half and use a wooden reamer to extract the juice into a bowl. To catch the seeds, place a mesh strainer over the bowl.

♔

Master Recipe

Homemade Mayonnaise

➤ NOTE: *Each time you add oil, make sure to whisk until it is thoroughly incorporated. It's fine to stop for a rest or to measure the next addition of oil. If the mayonnaise appears grainy or beaded after the last addition of oil, continue to whisk until smooth. See figures 10 and 11, page 35, for tips on making mayo. Makes about ¾ cup.*

1	large egg yolk
¼	teaspoon salt
¼	teaspoon Dijon-style mustard
1½	teaspoons lemon juice
1	teaspoon white wine vinegar
¾	cup corn oil

Master Instructions

1. Whisk egg yolk vigorously in medium bowl for 15 seconds. Add all remaining ingredients except for oil and whisk until yolk thickens and color brightens, about 30 seconds.

2. Add ¼ cup oil in slow, steady stream, continuing to whisk vigorously until oil is incorporated completely and mixture thickens, about 1 minute. Add another ¼ cup oil in the same manner, whisking until incorporated completely, about 30 seconds more. Add last ¼ cup oil all at once and whisk until incorporated completely, about 30 seconds more. Serve. (Can be refrigerated in airtight container for several days.)

■■ V A R I A T I O N S :

Lemon Mayonnaise

Add 1½ teaspoons grated lemon zest along with lemon juice.

Dijon Mayonnaise

Whisk 2 tablespoons Dijon-style mustard into finished mayonnaise.

Tarragon Mayonnaise

Stir 1 tablespoon minced fresh tarragon leaves into finished mayonnaise.

Food Processor Mayonnaise

Use 1 whole large egg and double quantities of other ingredients in Master Recipe. Pulse all ingredients except oil in workbowl of food processor fitted with metal blade three or four times to combine. With machine running, add oil in thin steady stream through open feed tube until incorporated completely. (If food pusher has small hole in bottom, pour oil into pusher and allow to drizzle down into machine while motor is running.) This recipe yields 1½ cups mayonnaise.

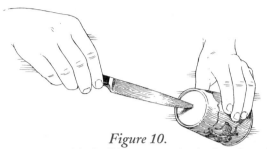

Figure 10.
An easy way to drizzle oil into mayonnaise slowly and evenly is
to punch a small hole in the bottom of a paper cup and use it to
add the oil to the egg yolk and lemon juice.

Figure 11.
Pour the oil into the cup while holding your finger over the hole,
then hold the cup above the bowl and remove your finger.
To keep the bowl stable while whisking, set it on a wet dishcloth.

chapter three

LEAFY SALADS

WHEN MAKING A LEAFY SALAD, CONSIDER how various greens will work together. There are times when you may want to use all tender lettuces and greens, such as Bibb and red oak. Other salads, especially those with chunky ingredients like sliced vegetables and fruits, cheese, or nuts, are better with a combination of tender and sturdier greens like arugula or radicchio.

In addition to texture, think about flavor. Balance peppery greens with mild greens, unless, of course, you are trying to create a very spicy salad that will served as a palate cleaner after a rich main course. Color should also be considered.

Master Recipe

Mixed Green Salad

➤ **NOTE**: *We like a hint of garlic in our basic salad but find the flavor is too bitter when minced garlic is added directly to the dressing. For garlic aroma without any harshness, we rub the salad bowl with a halved clove. See figures 12 and 13, page 39, for tips on coring and washing heads of lettuce. This salad serves four.*

½   medium garlic clove, peeled

2   quarts washed and dried mild salad greens, such as romaine, Boston, Bibb, or other leaf lettuces

¼   cup Classic Vinaigrette or any variation (*see* page 25)

■ INSTRUCTIONS:

1. Rub bottom and sides of large salad bowl (at least 4-quart) with garlic clove; discard garlic.

2. Place greens in large salad bowl. Drizzle dressing over greens and toss to coat. Serve immediately.

▪▪ VARIATIONS:

Tri-Color Salad with Balsamic Vinaigrette

Dress 4 cups arugula, 1 small head radicchio, cored and leaves torn, and 2 small heads Belgian endives, stems trimmed and leaves cut crosswise into thirds, with ¼ cup Balsamic Vinaigrette.

Asian Baby Greens with Orange-Sesame Vinaigrette

Dress 2 quarts baby spinach, mizuna, tatsoi, and/or other spicy Asian greens with ¼ cup Orange-Sesame Vinaigrette.

Arugula Salad with Walnut Vinaigrette and Toasted Walnuts

Dress 2 quarts arugula and 3 tablespoons toasted and coarsely chopped walnuts with ¼ cup Walnut Vinaigrette.

Figure 12.

To core and wash head lettuce simultaneously, rap the bottom of
the head of lettuce sharply on the counter to loosen the core. Turn
the head of lettuce over and pull out the core in one piece.

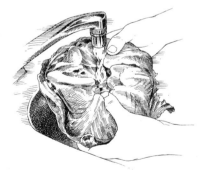

Figure 13.

Fill the hole left by the extracted core with water to rinse soil from
the lettuce. Separate leaves, wash again if necessary, and dry.

39

Caesar Salad

➤ **NOTE:** *Caesar dressing must be thick and smooth. Most recipes call for a raw egg, but we found that the dressing was thin with just one egg, and tended to separate when two were added. In the end, we found that coddling an egg (cooking it in the shell in simmering water for 45 seconds) releases its thickening powers and makes the creamiest, thickest Caesar dressing. Coddling does not kill any bacteria that may be present in eggs. See the variation on page 42 if you are concerned about eating raw eggs.*

If you don't own a garlic press, chop the garlic for both the croutons and dressing by hand; sprinkle it with salt and then continue mincing until quite fine. The garlic and anchovies in the dressing are optional, but most modern cooks would find the salad a bit bland without them. This salad yields four first-course servings.

Garlic Croutons

2   large garlic cloves, peeled and put through a garlic press

¼   teaspoon salt

3   tablespoons extra-virgin olive oil

2   cups ½-inch white bread cubes (from a baguette or country loaf)

Caesar Dressing

1   large egg

3   tablespoons lemon juice

1   teaspoon Worcestershire sauce

¼ teaspoon salt

8 grindings black pepper

1 small garlic clove, pressed (¼ teaspoon)

4 flat anchovy fillets, minced fine
   (scant 1½ teaspoons)

⅓ cup extra-virgin olive oil

2 medium heads romaine lettuce (large outer
   leaves removed) or 2 large romaine hearts,
   washed, dried, and torn into 1½-inch pieces
   (about 10 cups, lightly packed)

⅓ cup freshly grated Parmesan cheese

■ INSTRUCTIONS:

1. For croutons, preheat oven to 350 degrees. Mix garlic, salt, and oil in small bowl and set aside for 20 minutes. Spread bread cubes out over small baking sheet. Drizzle oil through fine-mesh strainer evenly onto bread and toss to coat. Bake until golden, about 12 minutes. Cool on baking sheet to room temperature. (Croutons can be stored in airtight container for 1 day.)

2. For dressing, bring several cups of water to boil in small saucepan. Carefully lower whole egg into water and cook for 45 seconds. Remove egg with slotted spoon. When cool enough to handle, crack egg into medium bowl. Add all other dressing ingredients except oil and whisk until smooth. Add oil in slow, steady stream, whisking constantly until smooth. Adjust seasonings. (Dressing may refrigerated in airtight container for 1 day; shake before using.)

3. Place lettuce in large bowl. Drizzle with half of dressing and toss to lightly coat leaves. Sprinkle with cheese, remaining dressing, and croutons and toss to coat evenly. Serve immediately.

▪▪ VARIATIONS:

Caesar Salad with Eggless Dressing

Because coddled eggs are not cooked long enough to kill any bacteria that might be present in the eggs, we tested a number of alternatives for people concerned about eating raw eggs. To our surprise, bland and smooth tofu is the perfect substitute for a coddled egg because it does not have any of the grittiness or sulfurous smell of hard-boiled eggs, the solution suggested in most books.

Substitute 2 ounces soft tofu, drained and crumbled (about ⅓ cup), for egg. Process dressing ingredients except oil in food processor until smooth, about 1 minute. With motor running, add oil in slow, steady stream until smooth.

Grilled Chicken Caesar Salad

This salad serves four as a main course. Brush two boneless, skinless chicken breasts (about ¾ pound) with 1 tablespoon olive oil and sprinkle with salt and pepper to taste. Grill or broil, turning once, until cooked through, about 10 minutes. Cool chicken to room temperature and slice crosswise into ½-inch-wide strips. Add chicken to salad along with cheese.

Bitter Green Salad with Citrus and Parmesan Shavings

➤ NOTE: *The combination of watercress and endive works well with the orange and grapefruit sections, although other greens, especially frisée, arugula, and dandelion, could also be used. Serve this refreshingly tart salad after a relatively high-fat meal like roast pork, duck, or goose. See figures 14–17 for information on sectioning oranges and grapefruits. This salad yields four servings.*

½	small red onion, diced fine
2	tablespoons red wine vinegar
⅓	cup extra-virgin olive oil
	Salt and ground black pepper
4	cups watercress, washed, stemmed, and dried
2	heads Belgian endive, cut into 2-inch pieces
1	large orange, peeled and sectioned, juice reserved
1	large grapefruit, peeled and sectioned, juice reserved
2	tablespoons chopped fresh parsley leaves
12	shavings Parmesan cheese

▟ INSTRUCTIONS:

1. Mix onion and vinegar in small bowl and let stand for 30 minutes. Whisk oil into onion mixture and season with salt and pepper to taste.

2. Mix watercress and endive in medium bowl. Add fruit and juices, onion mixture, and parsley; toss to coat. Divide among four salad plates. Garnish with cheese shavings and serve immediately.

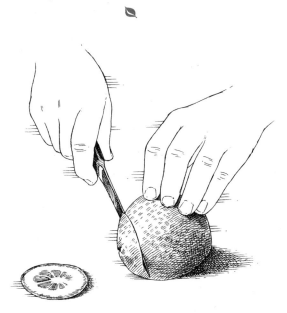

Figure 14.
To separate orange or grapefruit sections from the membranes that divide them, start by slicing a small section, about ½-inch thick, off the top and bottom ends of the fruit.

Figure 15.
With the fruit resting flat against a work surface, use a very
sharp paring knife to slice off the rind, including all of the bitter
white pith. Slide the knife edge from top to bottom of the fruit
and try to follow the outline of the fruit as closely as possible.

46

Figure 16.

Working over a bowl to catch the juice, slip the blade between a membrane and one section and slice to the center, separating one side of the section.

Figure 17.

Turn the blade of the knife so that it is facing out and is lined up along the membrane on the opposite side of the section. Slide the blade from the center out along the membrane to completely free the section. Continue until all the sections are removed.

47

Spinach Salad with Mushrooms, Croutons, and Warm Lemon Dressing

➤ NOTE: *Use a hunk of leftover baguette or country white bread to make the croutons for this recipe. This salad serves four. If you like, add 4 cooked and crumbled strips of bacon along with the croutons.*

1½	pounds flat-leaf spinach, stemmed, washed, dried, and torn into large pieces (about 9 cups)
½	pound fresh cremini or white mushrooms, cleaned, stems trimmed, and sliced thin
½	cup extra-virgin olive oil
3	cups stale bread, cut into ¾-inch cubes
2	medium garlic cloves, minced
¼	cup lemon juice
	Salt and ground black pepper

⁘ INSTRUCTIONS:

1. Place spinach and mushrooms in large bowl and set aside.

2. Heat oil in large skillet over medium-high heat until shimmering. Add bread and fry, turning several times with slotted spoon, until crisp and golden, about 3 minutes. Transfer croutons to plate lined with paper towel. Off heat, allow remaining oil to cool for 1 minute. Add garlic and cook until colored, about 2 minutes. Whisk in lemon juice and salt and pepper to taste. Pour warm dressing over salad and toss to coat. Add croutons, toss and serve immediately.

Watercress Salad with Pears, Walnuts, and Gorgonzola

➤ **NOTE:** *Pears, walnuts, and blue cheese are a classic combination, especially over bitter greens like watercress. Arugula and Stilton can stand in for the watercress and Gorgonzola. Toast the walnuts in a dry skillet over medium heat, shaking the pan occasionally, until fragrant, about 5 minutes. This salad serves four as an appetizer or after the main course in place of or before dessert.*

2	large, ripe but firm red pears, each halved, cored, and cut into 12 wedges
1	tablespoon lemon juice
6	cups arugula, stemmed, washed, and dried
½	cup Walnut Vinaigrette (*see* page 26)
3	ounces Gorgonzola cheese, crumbled
½	cup walnuts, toasted and chopped coarse
	Ground black pepper

⁝ INSTRUCTIONS:

1. Toss pear wedges with lemon juice in medium bowl; set aside.

2. Toss arugula with vinaigrette. Divide dressed greens among four salad plates. Arrange pears over greens, sprinkle with cheese, walnuts, and a generous grind of pepper. Serve immediately.

chapter four

❦

VEGETABLE SALADS

EGETABLE SALADS CAN BE DIVIDED INTO TWO classes based on the dressing. Creamy salads dressed with mayonnaise, such as coleslaw and potato salad, are perfect accompaniments to warm-weather meals because they can be refrigerated. Cucumber salads with a creamy yogurt dressing are related.

A second type of vegetable salad is dressed with vinaigrette. These dishes are generally best served at room temperature, when flavors are brightest. Also, unlike creamy mayonnaise-based salads, many vegetable salads that have been dressed with vinaigrette should be served immediately. This is especially true of green vegetables, which will lose their bright color and become soggy rather quickly.

Creamy Coleslaw

➤ NOTE: *Salting the cabbage and carrots draws off excess water that can otherwise cause the dressing to become watery. To keep the acidity in check, we prefer rice wine vinegar, which is less sour than other vinegars. If you like caraway or celery seed in your coleslaw, add ¼ teaspoon of either with the mayonnaise and vinegar. The cabbage can be prepared a day in advance, but dress it close to serving time. Serves four.*

1   pound (about ½ medium head) red or green cabbage, shredded fine or chopped to yield 6 cups (*see* figures 18–23, page 53)

1   large carrot, peeled and grated

2   teaspoons kosher salt or 1 teaspoon table salt

½   small onion, minced

½   cup Homemade Mayonnaise (*see* page 32) or store-bought

2   tablespoons rice wine vinegar
     Ground black pepper

░ INSTRUCTIONS:

1. Toss cabbage, carrots, and salt in colander set over medium bowl. Let stand until cabbage wilts, at least 1 hour and up to 4 hours.

2. Dump wilted cabbage and carrots into bowl. Rinse thoroughly in cold water (ice water if serving slaw immediately). Pour vegetables back into colander, pressing, but not squeezing on them to drain. Pat dry with paper towels. (Vegetables can be refrigerated in zipper-lock plastic bag overnight.)

3. Pour vegetables into bowl. Add onion, mayonnaise, and vinegar and toss to coat. Season with pepper to taste. Cover and refrigerate until ready to serve.

VARIATIONS:

Sweet-and-Sour Coleslaw
Toss cabbage, carrot, and salt with ½ cup sugar and let stand until wilted. Do not rinse vegetables. Replace onion and mayonnaise with ¼ teaspoon celery seeds and 6 tablespoons vegetable oil. Increase vinegar to ¼ cup. (Can be covered and refrigerated for 5 days.)

Curried Coleslaw with Apples and Raisins
Follow Sweet-and-Sour variation above, adding 1 teaspoon curry powder, 1 peeled and diced apple, and ¼ cup raisins along with oil and vinegar.

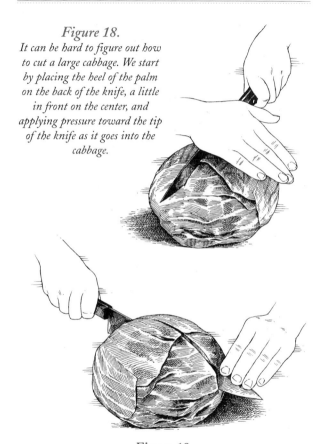

Figure 18.
It can be hard to figure out how to cut a large cabbage. We start by placing the heel of the palm on the back of the knife, a little in front on the center, and applying pressure toward the tip of the knife as it goes into the cabbage.

Figure 19.
Once the blade is completely below the top of the cabbage, move your fingers to the top of the front section of the knife and apply pressure to finish cutting.

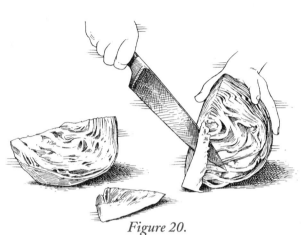

Figure 20.

For slicing cabbage by hand, use the following method to guarantee pieces that are the correct length. Cut the cabbage into quarters and remove the piece of the core attached to each quarter.

Figure 21.

Separate the cabbage quarters into stacks of leaves that flatten when pressed lightly.

Figure 22.
Use a chef's knife to cut each stack of cabbage diagonally (this ensures long pieces) into thin shreds. To chop cabbage, turn the pile of shredded cabbage crosswise, then cut the shreds into fine dice.

Figure 23.
For larger jobs, a food processor fitted with the shredding disk makes quick work of cabbage. Follow figures 18–21, rolling stacked leaves crosswise to fit them into the feed tube.

Boiled Potatoes for Salad

➤ **NOTE:** *Potato salad starts with boiled potatoes. In our testing, we found that low-starch potatoes such as Red Bliss provide the sturdy texture needed to stand up to dressing. Russet or baking potatoes will fall apart and produce a sloppy-looking salad. There's no need to salt the water for cooking the potatoes—in our tests we found that it does not penetrate. And make sure to cook the potatoes with their skins on to prevent them from becoming waterlogged. Cool the potatoes slightly, peel if desired, and then dress.*

2   **pounds Red Bliss or new potatoes
(about 6 medium or 18 new), rinsed
and scrubbed**

⠿ INSTRUCTIONS:

1. Place potatoes in 4- to 6-quart pot and cover with water. Bring to boil, cover, and simmer, stirring once or twice to ensure even cooking, until thin-bladed knife or metal cake tester inserted into a potato can be removed with no resistance, 25 to 30 minutes for medium potatoes and 15 to 20 minutes for new potatoes.

2. Drain and cool potatoes slightly. Peel if desired. Cut potatoes (use serrated knife if they have skins) as directed in following recipes while still warm, rinsing knife occasionally in warm water to remove gumminess. Proceed as directed in one of the following recipes.

Figure 24.
If you would like to keep the peel on the potatoes, use a serrated knife to slice the potatoes. Other knives will cause the skin to rip and shred.

American-Style Potato Salad with Eggs and Sweet Pickles

➤ **N O T E :** *Warm potatoes absorb vinegar best so sprinkle vinegar over them when still warm. Use sweet pickle, not relish for the best results in this recipe. Serves six to eight.*

1	recipe Boiled Potatoes for Salad (*see* page 56), cut into ¾-inch cubes
2	tablespoons red wine vinegar
½	teaspoon salt
½	teaspoon ground black pepper
3	hard-boiled eggs, peeled and cut into small dice
2	large scallions, sliced thin
1	small celery stalk, cut into small dice
¼	cup sweet pickle, cut into small dice
½	cup Homemade Mayonnaise (*see* page 32) or store-bought
2	tablespoons Dijon-style mustard
¼	cup minced fresh parsley leaves

⠿ I N S T R U C T I O N S :

1. Layer warm potato cubes in medium bowl, sprinkling with vinegar, salt, and pepper as you go. Refrigerate while preparing remaining ingredients.

2. Mix in remaining ingredients and refrigerate until ready to serve, up to 1 day.

French-Style Potato Salad with Tarragon Vinaigrette

➤ NOTE: *If fresh tarragon is not available, increase the parsley to three tablespoons and use tarragon vinegar in place of the white wine vinegar. Serves six.*

1	recipe Boiled Potatoes for Salad (*see* page 56), cut into ¼-inch-thick slices
2	tablespoons white wine vinegar
¼	teaspoon salt
¼	teaspoon ground black pepper
⅔	cup Tarragon-Mustard Vinaigrette (*see* page 27)
1	medium shallot, minced
2	tablespoons minced fresh parsley leaves

■■ INSTRUCTIONS:

1. Layer warm potato slices in medium bowl, sprinkling with vinegar and salt and pepper as you go. Let stand at room temperature while preparing dressing.

2. Whisk dressing and shallot together in small bowl. Pour over potatoes and toss lightly to coat. Refrigerate salad until ready to serve, up to 1 day. Bring to room temperature, stir in parsley, and serve.

German-Style Potato Salad with Bacon and Balsamic Vinegar

➤ **N O T E :** *Smaller new potatoes are more attractive in this recipe. The slices are smaller and tend not to break up as much as bigger potatoes do. Cider vinegar is more traditional, but we like the sweeter, fuller flavor of the balsamic vinegar. Serves six.*

1	recipe Boiled Potatoes for Salad (*see* page 56), cut into ¼-inch-thick slices
¼	cup balsamic or cider vinegar
½	teaspoon salt
½	teaspoon ground black pepper
4-5	slices bacon (about 4 ounces), cut crosswise into ¼-inch strips
1	medium onion, diced
2	tablespoons vegetable oil, if needed
½	cup beef broth
¼	cup minced fresh parsley leaves

▪▪ I N S T R U C T I O N S :

1. Layer warm potato slices in medium bowl, sprinkling with 2 tablespoons vinegar and salt and pepper as you go. Let stand at room temperature while preparing dressing.

2. Fry bacon in medium skillet over medium heat until brown and crisp, 7 to 10 minutes. Transfer bacon with slotted spoon to bowl of potatoes. Add onion to bacon drippings and sauté until softened, 4 to 5 minutes. If necessary, add oil to yield 2 tablespoons unabsorbed fat.

3. Add beef broth and bring to boil. Stir in remaining 2 tablespoons vinegar. Remove from heat and pour mixture over potatoes. Add parsley and toss gently to coat. Serve warm or tepid. (Salad may be covered and set aside at room temperature for several hours.)

Salted Cucumbers for Salad

➤ NOTE: *Cucumbers are so watery that they will dilute dressings unless salted. In our tests, we found that weighting the cucumbers maximizes the amount of the liquid they shed, as does time, at least up to a point. Cucumbers should be weighted for at least an hour, but after three hours they will not yield any additional liquid. Do not use more salt than directed below; even if rinsed off the cucumbers will still taste too salty.*

3   medium cucumbers (about 1½ pounds),
      peeled, halved lengthwise, seeded, and cut on
      the diagonal ¼-inch thick (*see* figures 25 and 26)

1   tablespoon salt

▮ INSTRUCTIONS:

Toss cucumbers with salt in strainer or colander set over bowl. Weight with water-filled, gallon-sized zipper-lock freezer bag, sealed tight (*see* figure 27). Drain for at least 1 hour, and up to 3 hours. Transfer cucumber to medium bowl and reserve for future use.

Yogurt Mint Cucumber Salad

➤ **NOTE:** *Known as raita, this creamy cucumber salad is traditionally served with curry as a cooling contrast. Serves four.*

1	cup plain low-fat yogurt
2	tablespoons extra-virgin olive oil
¼	cup minced fresh mint leaves
2	small garlic cloves, minced
	Salt and ground black pepper
1	recipe Salted Cucumbers for Salad (*see* page 62)

INSTRUCTIONS:

Whisk yogurt, oil, mint, garlic, and salt and pepper to taste in medium bowl. Add cucumbers and toss to coat. Serve chilled.

Figure 25.
Use a small spoon to remove the seeds and surrounding liquid from each cucumber half.

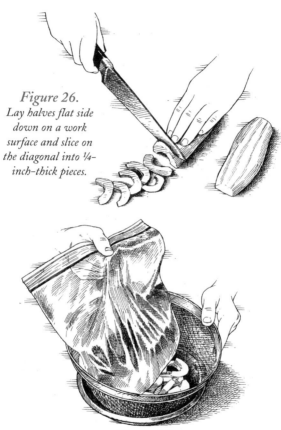

Figure 26.
Lay halves flat side
down on a work
surface and slice on
the diagonal into ¼-
inch-thick pieces.

Figure 27.
Weight the salted cucumber to help extract the liquid. To apply
the weight evenly, fill a gallon-size plastic bag with water and
seal tightly. Place the bag over the cucumbers in the colander.

64

Sesame-Lemon Cucumber Salad

➤ N O T E : *Toast sesame seeds in dry skillet set over medium heat until fragrant and golden, 4 to 5 minutes. The Asian flavors in the dressing make this salad a natural accompaniment to stir-fries. Serves four.*

¼	cup rice wine vinegar
1	tablespoon lemon juice
2	tablespoons Asian sesame oil
2	teaspoons sugar
⅛	teaspoon dried red pepper flakes, or to taste
1	tablespoon sesame seeds, toasted
1	recipe Salted Cucumbers for Salad (*see* page 62)

■ I N S T R U C T I O N S :

Whisk all ingredients except cucumbers together in medium bowl. Add cucumbers and toss to coat. Serve chilled or at room temperature.

Asparagus Vinaigrette with Sieved Egg and Pickled Onions

➤ NOTE: *The pickled pink onions are an excellent contrast to the creamy hard-boiled eggs and vinaigrette. Only ¼ cup of pickled onions are needed for this salad. Use the remaining pickled onions in other salads or on sandwiches. For a simpler version of this salad, use asparagus, hard-boiled egg, and ½ cup Tarragon-Mustard Vinaigrette (see page 27). Or try this salad with 1½ pounds of trimmed and steamed leeks.*

½	cup white wine vinegar, plus 1 tablespoon for vinaigrette
½	teaspoon sugar
	Salt and ground black pepper
1	small red onion, sliced thin and separated into rings
⅓	cup minced fresh parsley leaves
2	teaspoons minced fresh tarragon leaves
1	tablespoon drained capers
1	strip zest and 1 tablespoon juice from 1 small orange; zest sliced thin and blanched 10 seconds, then minced
½	teaspoon Dijon-style mustard
¼	cup extra-virgin olive oil
1½	pounds asparagus, tough ends snapped off
1	hard-boiled egg, peeled, white diced fine, yolk pushed through a sieve

INSTRUCTIONS:

1. Mix ½ cup vinegar, sugar, ½ teaspoon salt, and ¼ teaspoon pepper in nonreactive bowl. Place onion slices in colander in sink and pour boiling water over them. Add warm onions to vinegar mixture, adding enough cold water to cover. Let stand until onions are pink, about 15 minutes. Set aside.

2. Put parsley, tarragon, capers, and orange zest in small bowl with pinch of salt; stir in juice and remaining 1 tablespoon vinegar. Whisk in mustard, then slowly whisk in oil. Adjust seasonings and set aside.

3. Bring 1 inch water to boil in soup kettle. Put asparagus in steamer basket, then carefully place basket in kettle. Cover and steam until asparagus spears bend slightly when picked up, 4 to 5 minutes. Transfer asparagus to clean towel to dry.

4. Arrange asparagus on platter. Spoon vinaigrette over spears. Lift ¼ cup or so of onion rings from liquid and scatter over asparagus. Sprinkle diced egg white and sieved yolk over asparagus and serve immediately.

chapter five

GRAIN & BEAN
SALADS

ALADS MADE FROM PASTA, BULGUR, RICE, BREAD, and legumes are increasingly popular, especially during the warm weather. These salads are fairly hearty and can be served as side dishes or as light meals or lunches.

We have never been fans of mayonnaise-based macaroni salads. Pasta is too delicate to be sauced with something so heavy and creamy, especially if the pasta is refrigerated and eaten cold. But there are other styles of pasta salad that can be refreshing and delicious. Raw tomato sauces, vinaigrettes, and pesto are excellent dressings for pasta salads and all three types are discussed in this chapter.

Bread Salad with Tomatoes, Herbs, and Red Onions

➤ **NOTE:** *Sturdy Italian or coarse peasant bread is essential for this recipe, called panzanella in Italian. Serves four.*

1	pound day-old bread, crusts removed and torn into 1-inch cubes (about 6 cups)
½	cup extra-virgin olive oil
3	tablespoons red wine vinegar
2	large tomatoes, cored, seeded, and chopped
½	red onion, sliced paper-thin
2	tablespoons torn fresh basil or mint leaves
2	teaspoons whole fresh oregano leaves
1	tablespoon minced fresh parsley leaves
½	teaspoon salt
¼	teaspoon ground black pepper

INSTRUCTIONS:

1. Place bread cubes in shallow bowl. Mix oil, vinegar, tomatoes, onion, and half of herbs in medium bowl. Let stand for 10 minutes to develop flavors and then add to bread, along with remaining herbs, and mix well. Season with salt and pepper to taste.

2. If bread still seems dry, sprinkle with 1 to 2 tablespoons water. Serve. (If very sturdy bread is used, salad can be covered and set aside for up to 2 hours.)

Pasta Salad with Raw Tomato Sauce

➤ **N O T E :** *Raw tomatoes make an excellent base for pasta salads. The heat from the pasta slightly cooks diced tomatoes (as well as any raw garlic) but does not loosen the skins, which therefore do not need to be removed. The seeds, however, make pasta salad too watery and should be removed.*

If you like, prepare the tomatoes several hours in advance but wait to add the seasonings. The garlic will become too pungent and the salt will draw precious juices out of the tomatoes if the sauce marinates for more than half an hour or so.

Choose a short, stubby pasta that can trap bits of the sauce. Fusilli is an especially good choice, as is farfalle and orecchiette. Serves six to eight as a side dish. Do not refrigerate this salad; the cold will damage the flavor and texture of the tomatoes.

2	pounds ripe tomatoes
¼	cup extra-virgin olive oil
1	garlic clove, minced (about 1 teaspoon)
2	tablespoons minced fresh basil leaves
	Salt and ground black pepper
1	pound pasta (*see* note above)

⠿ I N S T R U C T I O N S :

1. Core and halve tomatoes crosswise. Use your fingers to push out seeds and surrounding gelatinous material. Cut seeded tomatoes into ½-inch dice and place in bowl large enough to hold cooked pasta. (Tomatoes can be covered and set aside for several hours.)

7 0

2. Bring 4 quarts of water to boil for cooking pasta. Add oil, garlic, basil, ¾ teaspoon salt, and several grindings of pepper to tomatoes and mix well. Add pasta and 1 tablespoon salt to boiling water and cook pasta until al dente. Drain well and immediately toss with tomato sauce. Cool to room temperature. Serve or cover with plastic and set aside for up to 4 hours.

VARIATIONS:

Pasta Salad with Raw Tomatoes, Olives, and Capers
Add ⅓ cup pitted, sliced Kalamata olives, 2 tablespoons drained capers, and ½ teaspoon hot red pepper flakes (optional) along with oil.

Pasta Salad with Raw Tomatoes and Mozzarella
Toss 6 ounces shredded fresh mozzarella cheese (about 1½ cups) with hot drained pasta and tomato sauce.

Pasta Salad with Broccoli and Olives

➤   N O T E : *This style of pasta salad, common in delis and gourmet stores, uses a vinaigrette to dress noodles. Often, finely diced or shredded vegetables are added. The problem with most of these pasta salads is the acid. Without any lemon or vinegar, the pasta salad tastes flat. But the acid often causes the pasta to soften and dulls the color and flavor of many vegetables, especially green ones. The solution is to use lemon juice, which is less acidic than vinegar, and to let the vegetables cool to room temperature to set their color before combining them with the hot pasta and dressing.*

Choose a short, stubby pasta that can trap pieces of vegetable such as fusilli, farfalle, orecchiette, or shells. Serves six to eight as a side dish.

1	large bunch broccoli (about 1½ pounds), stalks discarded and florets cut into small bite-sized pieces (about 5 cups)
	Salt
2	tablespoons lemon juice
½	teaspoon hot red pepper flakes
6	tablespoons extra-virgin olive oil
1	pound pasta
12	large black olives, pitted and chopped
12	large fresh basil leaves, shredded

⠿ I N S T R U C T I O N S :

1. Bring several quarts of water to boil for cooking broccoli. Add broccoli and salt to taste and cook until crisp-tender, about 2 minutes. Drain and cool to room temperature.

2. Whisk lemon juice, ¾ teaspoon salt, and hot red pepper flakes together in bowl large enough to hold cooked pasta. Whisk in oil until dressing is emulsified.

3. Bring 4 quarts of water to boil for cooking pasta. Add pasta and 1 tablespoon salt to boiling water and cook pasta until al dente. Drain well. Rewhisk dressing to emulsify and immediately toss with hot pasta, broccoli, olives, and basil. Cool to room temperature and serve. (Pasta salad can be refrigerated for 1 day. Bring to room temperature before serving.)

⠿ V A R I A T I O N :

Pasta Salad with Grilled Fennel and Red Onions

Omit broccoli and replace hot red pepper flakes with black pepper to taste and olives with 8 drained and slivered sun-dried tomatoes packed in oil. Trim 1 large fennel bulb and cut through base into ½-inch-thick wedges. Peel and cut 2 medium red onions crosswise into ½-inch-thick rounds. Brush vegetables with 1½ tablespoons olive oil and sprinkle with salt to taste. Grill, turning once, until both sides are marked with dark grill marks, about 15 minutes. Cool vegetables and cut into thin strips. Add to hot pasta and vinaigrette along with sun-dried tomatoes and basil.

Pasta Salad with Pesto

➤ **NOTE:** *Pesto is a natural sauce for pasta salad because of its concentrated flavor. But hot pasta can turn pesto sauce an unappealing greenish brown, a problem that becomes even more noticeable if the salad is set aside for some time before serving. In our testing, we found that adding some parsley to pesto helps keep its color green without affecting the flavor.*

If you like, add cooked and cooled vegetables to this recipe. Broccoli florets are especially good, as are tomatoes. About three cups of cooked vegetables are enough for a pound of pasta. This is one pasta salad that can tolerate the addition of meat. If you like, add two cups of shredded cooked chicken. Fusilli is our first choice when saucing with pesto. Serves six to eight as a side dish.

3	medium garlic cloves, threaded on a skewer
2	cups fresh packed basil leaves
¼	cup fresh flat Italian parsley leaves
¼	cup pine nuts, toasted
½	cup extra-virgin olive oil
	Salt
¼	cup finely grated Parmesan cheese
1	pound pasta

INSTRUCTIONS:

1. Bring small saucepan of water to boil. Lower skewered garlic into water; boil until garlic is partially blanched, about 45 seconds. Immediately run cold water over garlic to stop the cooking. Remove from skewer; peel and mince.

2. Place basil and parsley in heavy-duty, quart-size, zipper-lock plastic bag; pound with flat side of meat pounder until all leaves are bruised.

3. Place garlic, herbs, nuts, oil, and pinch of salt in bowl of food processor fitted with steel blade; process until smooth, stopping as necessary to scrape down bowl with flexible spatula.

4. Transfer mixture to bowl large enough to hold cooked pasta, stir in cheese, and adjust salt. Cover and set aside.

5. Bring 4 quarts of water to boil for cooking pasta. Add pasta and 1 tablespoon salt to boiling water and cook pasta until al dente. Drain well. Toss with pesto. Cool to room temperature and serve. (Pasta salad can be refrigerated for 1 day. Bring to room temperature before serving.)

Tabbooleh

➤ **NOTE:** *As is common in traditional Arab recipes, this grain salad contains more parsley than bulgur. We prefer a ratio of five parts parsley to three or four parts wheat, but you may adjust as you like. Soaking the bulgur in lemon juice (as opposed to water or vinaigrette) gives it a fresh, intense flavor without the added heaviness associated with the oil. Fine-grain bulgur is our first choice for this recipe but medium-grain is an acceptable substitute. Coarse bulgur must be cooked before it is eaten and cannot be used in this recipe. This salad serves four to six as a side dish.*

½   cup fine-grain bulgur wheat, rinsed and drained

⅓   cup lemon juice

⅓   cup extra-virgin olive oil
    Salt

⅛   teaspoon cayenne or Middle Eastern red pepper, optional

2   cups minced fresh parsley leaves

2   medium tomatoes, cored, halved, seeded, and cut into very small dice

4   medium scallions, green and white parts, minced

2   tablespoons minced fresh mint leaves or 1 rounded teaspoon dried mint

▛ INSTRUCTIONS:

1. Mix bulgur with ¼ cup lemon juice in medium bowl. Set aside, stirring occasionally, until grains are tender and fluffy, 20 to 40 minutes.

2. Whisk remaining lemon juice, oil, salt to taste, and cayenne, if using, together in small bowl. Add parsley, tomatoes, scallions, and mint to bulgur. Add dressing and toss to combine. Cover and refrigerate to let flavors blend, at least 1 hour and no more than 4 hours. Warm slightly at room temperature before serving.

French Lentil Salad with Caraway and Radish

➤ **NOTE:** *French green lentils take longer to cook than the standard brown variety but keep their shape better, making them the best choice for salads. Ignore warnings about not adding salt to legumes, especially lentils, as they cook. Although the salt may slightly slow down water absorption and add 5 or 10 minutes to the cooking time, it develops and strengthens the flavor of the lentils and should be added at the start along with the aromatics. Serve this hearty, piquant salad with grilled sausage, roast duck, or pâté. It works well as is or over a bed of salad greens. Serves four.*

1	cup French Le Puy lentils, picked over and rinsed
½	onion, halved and studded with 2 whole cloves
1	carrot, peeled and halved
1	celery stalk, cut into thirds
1	bay leaf
	Salt
2	tablespoons sherry vinegar
3	tablespoons whole-grain mustard
1	tablespoon caraway seeds, lightly crushed
2	garlic cloves, minced
	Ground black pepper
½	cup extra-virgin olive oil
4	radishes, minced
¼	cup minced fresh parsley leaves

■ INSTRUCTIONS:

1. Bring lentils, clove-studded onion, carrot, celery, bay leaf, ½ teaspoon salt, and 4 cups water to boil in medium saucepan. Boil for 5 minutes, reduce heat, and simmer until lentils are tender but still hold their shape, 25 to 30 minutes.

2. Meanwhile, mix vinegar, mustard, caraway seeds, garlic, and salt and pepper to taste in large bowl. Slowly whisk in oil to make vinaigrette; set aside.

3. Drain lentils, discarding vegetables and bay leaf. Add warm lentils to vinaigrette and toss to coat. Cool to room temperature. (Lentil salad can be covered and set aside for several hours). Stir in radishes and parsley and serve immediately.

chapter six

MAIN-COURSE SALADS

SALAD CAN BE BECOME DINNER WHEN PROTEIN IS added to the mix. For these salads, there are several points to remember. You want to use enough protein to make the salad seem substantial without overwhelming the greens. Somewhere between three and six ounces of protein per person is best.

Second, these salads are not the time to use tender Boston lettuce or tiny tatsoi. The greens must have enough crunch and flavor to stand up to the cooked protein, the vegetables, and tangy dressings used in these salads. Flat-leaf spinach is an excellent choice, as is watercress, arugula, mizuna, or escarole.

Spinach Salad with Shrimp, Mango, and Red Onion

➤ **NOTE:** *To save time, buy shrimp that has been peeled and cooked. If you want to boil the shrimp yourself, buy slightly more than one pound with the shells on. This salad serves four.*

1½	pounds flat-leaf spinach, stemmed, washed, dried, and torn into large pieces (about 9 cups)
1	pound cooked medium shrimp
1	large ripe mango, peeled, pitted, and cut into thin strips
½	small red onion, peeled and sliced thin
1	tablespoon rice wine vinegar
⅔	cup Orange-Sesame Vinaigrette (*see* page 27)

■ INSTRUCTIONS:

1. Place spinach, shrimp, and mango in large bowl and set aside.

2. Place onion and vinegar in small bowl. Macerate until onions are bright pink, about 5 minutes. Drain onions and add to salad bowl. Pour dressing over salad and toss gently. Serve immediately.

Spinach and Avocado Salad with Chili-Flavored Chicken

➤ N O T E : *A creamy yogurt dressing spiked with lemon and garlic is a good match for the strong flavors in this salad. This salad serves four.*

2	teaspoons chili powder
1	teaspoon ground cumin
	Salt
2	teaspoons vegetable oil
1	pound boneless, skinless chicken breasts, trimmed of excess fat
1½	pounds flat-leaf spinach, stemmed, washed, dried, and torn into large pieces (about 9 cups)
4	ripe plum tomatoes (about ¾ pound), cored and cut into wedges
1	Hass avocado, halved, pitted, peeled, and cut into thin strips (*see* figures 28–33)
3	tablespoons lemon juice
¾	cup plain yogurt
2	tablespoons extra-virgin olive oil
1	large garlic clove, minced

▓ I N S T R U C T I O N S :

1. Heat broiler or light grill. Combine chili powder, cumin, and ½ teaspoon salt in small bowl. Rub vegetable oil then spice mixture into both sides of each chicken breast. Broil or grill chicken, turning once, until cooked through, about 10 minutes. Set aside.

2. Place spinach and tomatoes in large bowl. Sprinkle avocado with 1 tablespoon lemon juice and add to salad bowl.

3. Whisk yogurt, olive oil, garlic, remaining 2 tablespoons lemon juice, and salt to taste in small bowl.

4. Slice chicken crosswise into ¾-inch-wide strips and add to salad bowl. Pour dressing over salad and toss gently. Serve immediately.

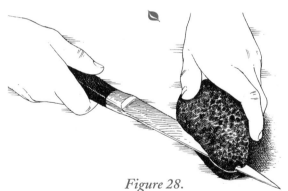

Figure 28.

With their dark, pebbly skin, Hass avocados are generally creamier and better in salads than larger, smooth-skinned varieties. To remove the flesh in neat slices, start by slicing around the pit and cutting through both ends.

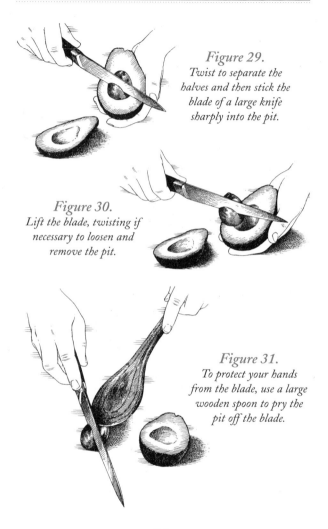

Figure 29.
Twist to separate the
halves and then stick the
blade of a large knife
sharply into the pit.

Figure 30.
Lift the blade, twisting if
necessary to loosen and
remove the pit.

Figure 31.
To protect your hands
from the blade, use a large
wooden spoon to pry the
pit off the blade.

Figure 32.
Use a small paring knife to slice through the meat, but not the skin.

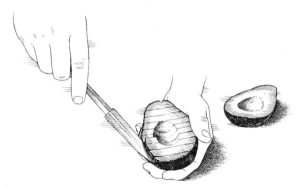

Figure 33.
Run a rubber spatula around the circumference, just inside the
skin, to loosen the meat, then twist the spatula to pop out the meat.

85

Escarole Salad with Bacon and Poached Eggs

➤ NOTE: *Poaching eggs can be a messy business, with simmering water causing the eggs to loose their shape and the whites to feather. We found that adding eggs to boiling water, then turning off the heat and covering the pan allows them to cook by residual heat without the problem of churning bubbles. For best results, use a deep skillet rather than a saucepan (the eggs will hit the bottom of the pan more quickly and set properly) and heavily salt the water for best flavor. This salad is a one-dish brunch and will serve four. For information on poaching eggs in advance, see figure 35.*

1	head escarole, washed, dried, and torn into pieces (about 8 cups)
1	teaspoon salt
2	tablespoons distilled white vinegar
4	large eggs, each cracked into a small handled cup
⅔	cup Creamy Vinaigrette (*see* page 27)
4	strips bacon, cooked, drained, and crumbled
12	cherry tomatoes, halved
2	ounces Roquefort cheese, crumbled
2	tablespoons minced fresh chervil or parsley leaves

▪▪ INSTRUCTIONS:

1. Place escarole in large bowl and set aside.

2. Fill 8- to 10-inch nonstick skillet nearly to rim with water, adding salt and vinegar. Bring to boil over high heat. Lower lips of each cup just into water at once; tip eggs into boiling water (*see* figure 34, page 88), cover, and remove pan from heat. Poach until yolks are medium-firm, exactly 4 minutes. For firmer yolks (or for extra-large or jumbo eggs), poach for 4½ minutes; for looser yolks (or for medium eggs), poach for 3 minutes.

3. While eggs are poaching, toss greens with vinaigrette. Divide greens among four plates.

4. With slotted spoon, carefully lift and drain each egg over skillet. Slide one egg onto each plate along with portion of bacon, tomato, cheese, and herb. Serve immediately.

Figure 34.

To get four eggs into simmering water at the same time, crack
each into a small cup with a handle. Lower lips of each cup just
into the water at same time and then tips eggs into the pan.

Figure 35.

Poaching eggs does not have to require last-minute work. If you
prefer, place cooked eggs in bowl with enough ice water to submerge
them, then refrigerate for up to 3 days. When ready to serve, use a
slotted spoon to transfer each egg to a skillet filled with boiling
water. Turn off the heat, cover, and wait 20 to 30 seconds. Use a
slotted spoon to remove eggs and proceed with recipe.

Thai-Style Charred Beef Salad

➤ **NOTE**: *Tender, inexpensive flank steak is grilled then sliced thin and tossed with a hot-and-sweet Thai-style dressing, cucumber, red onion, leafy greens, and fresh aromatic herbs. Cut the flank steak in half lengthwise before grilling it to keep sliced pieces to a reasonable length. A whole steak usually weighs just under two pounds, which is too much for a salad for four. Reserve the smaller piece for stir-fries or other salads. The fiery dressing can be made with any fresh chile or crushed red pepper flakes, or a combination, as we have done.*

1¼	pounds flank steak, cut in half lengthwise
2	teaspoons extra-virgin olive oil
	Salt and ground black pepper
½	cup rice wine vinegar
2½	tablespoons sugar
⅛	teaspoon crushed red pepper flakes
1	medium cucumber, peeled, halved lengthwise, seeded, and cut on the diagonal ¼-inch thick (*see* figures 25 and 26, page 63)
½	small red onion, sliced very thin
1	small jalapeño or other fresh chile, stemmed, seeded, and cut into paper-thin rounds
4	cups Boston or Bibb lettuce, washed, thoroughly dried, and torn into large pieces
1	tablespoon fresh cilantro leaves, torn
1	tablespoon fresh mint leaves, torn

▚ **INSTRUCTIONS:**

1. Light charcoal or gas grill. Brush flank steak with olive oil and season generously with salt and pepper to taste. Grill steak over very hot fire until medium-rare, about 5 minutes per side. Remove steak from grill, let rest for 5 minutes, and slice thinly across the grain into ¼-inch-thick strips. Set steak aside.

2. Meanwhile, bring ⅔ cup water and vinegar to boil in small nonreactive saucepan over medium heat. Stir in sugar to dissolve. Reduce heat, add crushed red pepper flakes, and simmer until slightly syrupy, about 15 minutes. Cool to room temperature.

3. Combine steak, cucumber, onion, and chile in medium bowl. Pour cooled dressing over steak and vegetables and toss to coat.

4. Arrange salad greens over large platter. Spoon steak and vegetables over greens and drizzle with any dressing left in bowl. Sprinkle with torn herbs and serve immediately.

Roast Chicken Breasts for Salad

➤ **NOTE**: *In our testing, we found that chicken cooked for salad by wet methods (steaming, poaching, roasting in foil, or microwaving), produces bland meat with an unpleasant boiled chicken flavor. The dry heat of roasting results in more flavorful, firmer meat. Shredding the cooked and cooled chicken by hand gives the meat an uneven texture and helps the dressing cling to each piece.*

> **2** large whole bone-in, skin-on chicken breasts
> (at least 1½ pounds each)
> **1** tablespoon vegetable oil
> Salt

INSTRUCTIONS:

1. Adjust oven rack to middle position and heat oven to 400 degrees. Set breasts on small, foil-lined jelly roll pan. Brush with oil and sprinkle generously with salt.

2. Roast until thermometer inserted into thickest part of breast registers 160 degrees, 35 to 40 minutes. Cool to room temperature, remove skin, and shred according to figures 36–39, page 92.

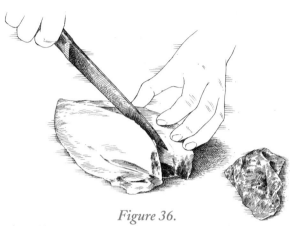

Figure 36.

Once chicken breasts have cooled, remove the skin and then slice
along the center bone to separate the two pieces of the breast meat.

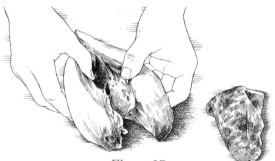

Figure 37.

Insert your fingers into the cut made by the knife and gently pry
the breast meat off the bone in two pieces.

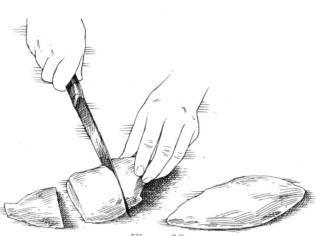

Figure 38.
Cut each breast into thirds with a sharp knife.

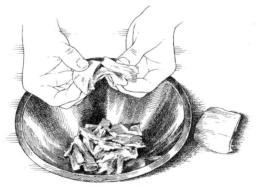

Figure 39.
Use your hands to pull apart breast pieces and shred into small pieces.

Classic Creamy Chicken Salad

➤ **NOTE:** *In addition to the parsley, add 2 tablespoons minced fresh tarragon or basil leaves if you like. This recipe begins with about 5 cups of shredded chicken, enough for 6 servings. Use this salad to make sandwiches or serve over a bed of leafy greens.*

1	recipe Roast Chicken Breasts for Salad (*see* page 91)
2	medium celery stalks, diced small
2	medium scallions, white and green parts, minced
¾	cup Homemade Mayonnaise (*see* page 32) or store-bought
2	tablespoons lemon juice
2	tablespoons minced fresh parsley leaves
	Salt and ground black pepper

INSTRUCTIONS:

Mix all ingredients, including salt and pepper to taste, in large bowl. Serve immediately or refrigerate for up to 1 day.

VARIATIONS:

Waldorf Chicken Salad

Add 1 large crisp apple, cored and cut into medium dice, and 6 tablespoons chopped, toasted walnuts.

Curried Chicken Salad with Raisins and Honey

Add 6 tablespoons golden raisins, 2 teaspoons curry powder, and 1 tablespoon honey. Use cilantro in place of parsley.

Chicken Salad with Hoisin Dressing

➤ NOTE: *Try serving this Asian-style salad on a bed of spinach leaves with sliced cucumber and radishes, or rolled in a flour tortilla with shredded iceberg lettuce or watercress. Serves six.*

1	recipe Roast Chicken Breasts for Salad (*see* page 91)
2	medium celery stalks, diced small
2	medium scallions, white and green parts, minced
2	tablespoons minced fresh cilantro or parsley leaves
¾	cup Hoisin Vinaigrette (*see* page 28)

▞ INSTRUCTIONS:

Mix chicken, celery, scallions, and cilantro in large bowl. Add dressing and toss to coat. Serve immediately or refrigerate for up to 1 day.

❦

i n d e x